Frenemies

Dealing with Friend Drama

ABDO
Publishing Company

Strong, Beautiful Girls

Frenemies

Dealing with Friend Drama

by Lisa L. Owens

Content Consultant
Dr. Robyn J. A. Silverman
Child/Teen Development Expert and Success Coach
Powerful Words Character Development

Credits

Published by ABDO Publishing Company, 8000 West 78th Street, Edina, Minnesota 55439. Copyright © 2010 by Abdo Consulting Group, Inc. International copyrights reserved in all countries. No part of this book may be reproduced in any form without written permission from the publisher. The Essential Library™ is a trademark and logo of ABDO Publishing Company.

Printed in the United States.

Editor: Amy Van Zee
Copy Editor: Melissa Johnson
Interior Design and Production: Becky Daum
Cover Design: Becky Daum

Library of Congress Cataloging-in-Publication Data
Owens, L. L.
  Frenemies : dealing with friend drama / by L.L. Owens ; content consultant, Robyn J. A. Silverman.
    p. cm. — (Essential health : strong, beautiful girls)
  Includes index.
  ISBN 978-1-60453-750-5
  1. Interpersonal relations in adolescence. 2. Teenage girls—Psychology. 3. Female friendship. 4. Interpersonal conflict in adolescence. I. Title.

  BF724.3.I58O94 2010
  155.5'33—dc22
                                        2009002132

Contents

Meet Dr. Robyn

Dr. Robyn Silverman loves to spend time with young people. It's what she does best! As a child and adolescent development specialist, Dr. Robyn has devoted her time to helping girls just like you become all they can be. Throughout the Strong, Beautiful Girls series, you'll hear her expert advice as she offers wisdom on boy-friends, school, and everything in between.

An award-winning body image expert and the creator of the Powerful Words Character System, Dr. Robyn likes to look on the bright side of life. She knows how tough it is to be a young woman in today's world, and she's prepared with encouragement to help you embrace your beauty even when your "frenemies" tell you otherwise. Dr. Robyn struggled with her own body image while growing up, so she knows what you're going through.

Dr. Robyn has been told she has a rare talent—to help girls share their wildest dreams and biggest problems. Her compassion makes her a trusted friend to many girls, and she considers it a gift to be able to interact with the young people who she sees as the leaders of tomorrow. She even started a girls' group, the Sassy Sisterhood Girls Circle, to help young women pinpoint how media messages impact their lives and body confidence so they can get healthy and get happy.

As a speaker and a success coach, her powerful messages have reached thousands of people. Her expert advice has been featured in *Prevention* magazine, *Parents* magazine, and the *Washington Post*. She was even a guest editor for the Dove Self-Esteem Fund: Campaign for Real Beauty. But she has an online presence too, and her writing can be found through her blogs, www.DrRobynsBlog.com and www.BodyImageBlog.com, or through her Web site, www.DrRobynSilverman.com. Dr. Robyn also enjoys spending time with her family in Massachusetts.

Dr. Robyn believes that young people are assets to be developed, not problems to be fixed. She's out to help you become the best you can be. As she puts it, "I'm stepping up to the plate to highlight news stories gone wrong, girls gone right, and programs that help to support strengths instead of weaknesses. I'd be grateful if you'd join me."

Take It from Me

I'm thrilled to share this book about friendship issues with you! The situations I've highlighted reflect a sampling of the wide variety of real-life dramas unfolding among friends all over the world—and probably in your own school—right now. You'll read about catching friends doing the wrong thing, breaking away from old friends, changing the terms of a friendship, stepping in to keep a friend safe, and more.

Conflict among friends can arise in any number of circumstances. I was lucky to have a lot of good friends as a young girl. But like every girl my age, I lived through all sorts of conflicts with my friends—from minor issues we resolved in a snap to bigger conflicts that left lasting memories. I'll never forget the sting of a best friend dropping me for someone new. I remember the hurt in a friend's eyes and the pain it caused me after I'd played a spiteful joke just to get even. I also recall feeling anxious (but good) about stepping up to help one friend, knowing it meant confronting and possibly losing another. And I can think of many times when a good friend and I disagreed about the small stuff, such as what to do or how to do it, but found a way to deal with it and get back to having fun together.

On the sometimes bumpy road to adult-hood, every girl learns how to navigate the different relationships she forms with her friends. Using observational skills, common sense, and good old-fashioned trial and error, she figures out how to read others' behavioral clues. She learns to adjust her communication style, assert herself, give and receive support, think about others' feelings, and—ultimately—build meaningful, long-lasting friendships. And isn't that the point?

Trust me, if you haven't already, you will experience your fair share of friend drama over the next few years. You may suffer betrayals, engage in petty disagreements, and even lose a friend or two. You can expect to be wronged and to make your own mistakes. But I promise you, the tough times will all be worth it. I know that with an open mind and a willingness to change and grow, you can get through all of it and come out on the other side still smiling with a healthy group of true friends to call your own.

XOXO,
Lisa

1

Fitting In

Wanting to fit in with new friends is natural. Many times, fitting in happens easily, such as when you meet someone and find out that you both love black licorice, funky jewelry, hip-hop, or Jane Austen. It feels great to make strong connections with other people. When that happens, you immediately feel more comfortable. You feel that you belong somewhere and that others understand you.

Sometimes in life, though, the process of fitting in doesn't go as smoothly as you might like. You feel as if you have to put in extra effort to make it happen. In some cases, you won't fit in and will just move on. But in others, you might alter the way you look or act so you impress that friend or blend in with that group you want to join.

Making personal changes is not always a bad idea. It may work out well. But if you make drastic changes to fit in with a new group of kids, an old friend may not like the new you. Or she may not understand your need to change. In some cases, she may be right. That's what Carly found out.

Carly's Story

Carly was nervous about starting seventh grade. Her family had moved to a new neighborhood in their city over the summer. That meant she would attend a different school than most of her old classmates.

But on the first day of school, Carly was relieved to see Simone, a friend from sixth grade, sitting in her homeroom class. Knowing even one person helped Carly feel less alone.

Carly and Simone stuck together at first. Soon they each started making their own friends. Carly met people by joining the swim team and the choir. Simone wasn't into sports or music. She met someone in class who introduced her to a group of girls known as the Delinquents. They just called themselves that to be funny. They didn't cause any problems. But they did share a dislike for school activities and the kids who joined them.

Knowing even one person helped Carly feel less alone.

At lunch every day, Simone's new friends took over the east corner of the cafeteria. After school, they'd all walk over to the nearby arcade to hang out until dinnertime. Simone never invited Carly to tag along, but Carly didn't mind. She enjoyed her new friends and wanted Simone to enjoy hers. Besides, she and Simone still saw each other and talked.

But Carly noticed Simone changing as the weeks went by. Soon Simone dressed, acted, and talked exactly like the rest of the Delinquents. She was friendly to Carly in private, but if one of her new friends was around, she acted like she hardly knew Carly—or worse, that she could barely tolerate her.

Talk About It

- **Have you ever watched a friend start acting like other kids in a group? What did you think about it?**

- **Have you ever changed yourself to fit in? Did it work out for you?**

At a school assembly one morning, Carly saw Simone enter the auditorium. She waved and pointed to the empty seat next to her. Simone clearly saw Carly. She blushed and quickly looked away. When she spotted the other Delinquents, she hurried over to sit with them, completely ignoring Carly as she passed.

That was the last straw for Carly. She decided to stop by Simone's house that night.

"What are you doing here?" Simone asked when she opened the door.

"I came to see my friend Simone," Carly said. "*If* she still lives here. I'm not sure I'd recognize her anymore."

Talk About It

- Have you ever pretended not to see a friend? Why did you do it? How would you feel if your friend pretended not to see you?

- What do you think was going on in Simone's head when she ignored Carly?

"Very funny. I'm kinda busy right now, Carly," Simone said.

"Oh, well, then I guess I've got my answer," Carly replied. She turned to walk away.

"What are you talking about?" Simone asked.

Carly looked Simone straight in the eye as she said, "It's obvious you don't want to be friends anymore, Simone."

"I never said that!" Simone protested.

Simone stared at the ground. She'd been feeling guilty about ignoring Carly, and now she knew Carly was upset.

"You flat-out ignored me at the assembly today. You act like you're embarrassed to know me or something. What's going on with you?"

Simone stared at the ground. She'd been feeling guilty about ignoring Carly, and now she knew Carly was upset. "Hey, Carly, I'm sorry," she said. "I know I've been rude. It's just that the Delinquents wouldn't understand why I'm friends with you. They hate kids

who do sports and things. They think all that stuff is so lame."

"Do *you* think it's lame?" Carly said.

"No, of course not. But they don't want to hear what I think," Simone said.

"Then why do you want to hang out with them?" Carly asked. "I've never seen you act so afraid to be yourself before."

"I just want them to like me," Simone mumbled.

"It sure looks like they like you. If they're really your friends, those girls aren't going to hate you just for talking to me," Carly said. "They probably don't even care. And if they do, well, maybe you're better off without them. Our school has tons of kids who would love to be friends with you. Me included."

"You're right," Simone sighed. "I've been acting crazy. Honest, Carly, I don't want to stop being friends."

"Prove it," Carly challenged. "Eat lunch at my table tomorrow. If your friends ask you to join them, just say you can't because you're eating with me. What are they going to do?"

"They might stop talking to me," Simone said.

"So what if they do?" Carly asked. "Anyway, if you don't start acting like my friend again, I'll *definitely* stop talking to you."

"Seriously?" Simone said.

"Seriously," Carly said. "But don't worry. It will all work out. You'll see."

Talk About It

- Is it a good idea for Simone to acknowledge her friendship with Carly in front of the other kids? Why or why not?

- Do you think Simone will gain enough confidence to be herself?

- How would you describe Carly's handling of the situation with Simone?

As Simone made major changes, Carly noticed that Simone stopped acting like herself. Why did Simone change? For a fairly common reason, really: Simone desperately wanted to fit in. So much so that she was willing to change everything about herself.

In general, learning to fit in and get along with others is an important part of making friends. But fitting in at all costs is rarely the answer. If you change who you are in order to fit in, your new "friends" will like you for everything that you really aren't. Erasing your own personality and then substituting it with someone else's idea of what you should be might feel like a good solution in the short term. But you probably won't be able to keep it up for long. Eventually, your true self will want to emerge, and that is bound to cause conflict with the friends you worked so hard to win over. Plus, wouldn't you rather have friends who like you for you?

One of the best ways to attract friends is to maintain your unique identity. When you give yourself permission to think and act on your own terms, you can always feel sure that your friends like you for you.

Get Healthy

1. Recognize that friends worth having will like you for who you are. Their friendship won't depend on if you look or think like them.

2. Always keep in mind that you deserve just as much respect as anyone else. Someone who will only be your friend if you change yourself probably doesn't respect you. She may not come through for you when you actually need a friend to lean on.

3. If you're considering making changes to please a new friend, ask yourself some of these questions: Are these changes I want to make? Do I really need to be different, or am I okay the way I am? Does this friend expect me to change—and, if so, is the friendship more important than my own identity?

The Last Word from Lisa

Every young girl wants to fit in with a group. If you find yourself in a situation where someone wants you to change to be her friend, take a step back. Maybe she needs to accept you as you are, or maybe you don't need her as a friend after all. Also, be sure to think it over before dumping a proven friend for a new one. Real friends are hard to come by, so it's worth trying hard to keep the ones you already have.

2

Trash Talking

Most teens know a thing or two about trash talking. Insulting other kids behind their backs is something many do just for fun. No doubt you've heard plenty of trash talk, and you've probably done it, too. Maybe you didn't like the person you were putting down. Maybe you were mad at someone who'd been trash talking about you. Or maybe you were just bored and felt like stirring things up.

Trash talking can take many forms. See if the following examples ring any bells. Several kids at the bus stop gossip about their friend cheating on a test. Someone passes a note about the new guy's strange accent. Two friends spend hours on the phone dissecting another friend's hideous wardrobe. Or, a popular girl posts insults on her blog about the weird girl from fifth-period study hall.

Do any of these situations sound familiar? Trash talking can seem harmless, and even funny—especially when you're the one talking trash or acting as a willing audience. But consider this: What happens when a target hears the terrible things someone has been saying about her? What if you get caught and your target is actually a friend you don't want to lose? Trash

Trash talking can cause lots of hurt feelings and create some real problems for everyone involved.

talking can cause lots of hurt feelings and create some real problems for everyone involved. Just take it from Gina, who learned her lesson the hard way.

Gina's Story

Gina and Hallie grew up in the same neighborhood. They always lived just a few doors away from each other and had been close friends since they were in preschool.

So naturally, Gina was really happy when Hallie won the lead role in the school play. To celebrate, Gina treated Hallie to an ice-cream sundae with the works. Before long, though, Hallie got super busy with re-hearsals. And "the play" was the only thing Hallie ever wanted to talk about. Each morning on their way to school, Gina listened to full recaps of the previous night's play practice. Hallie shared every last detail, distractedly twirling her hair as she spoke. She often went on and on, never even noticing that Gina didn't laugh at the hilarious private cast jokes she told—or that Gina rarely said much of anything.

Talk About It

- Is Gina still happy about Hallie's involvement with the play? How can you tell?

- Have you ever went on and on about a fun new activity while you were talking to a friend? What was your friend's reaction?

- Have you ever pretended to be interested in a friend's stories when you really weren't? How would you feel if a friend did that to you?

Gina and Hallie seldom saw each other outside of school anymore. When they did, Gina felt frustrated that Hallie was always rushing off to study her lines or get fitted for costumes. She missed talking to Hallie about homework, parents, cute guys, and other stuff. She missed having Hallie listen to *her* stories and laugh at *her* jokes. Gina couldn't wait for the day she'd never have to hear another word about Hallie's play.

One Thursday afternoon after her Spanish Club meeting, Gina was talking with the other club

members. Gina had no idea that Hallie was on her way to find her.

Talk About It

- Have you ever missed a friend who became busy with something new? What did you do about it?

- Does Gina have a right to feel frustrated with her friend? Do you think that she might be a little jealous of Hallie? Why or why not?

- Do you think Hallie is aware that she talks so much about the play? Should Gina tell her how she feels?

Hallie had just finished dress rehearsal and decided to try to catch Gina. She hoped to walk home with her. Hallie was excited for opening night tomorrow. As she made her way toward the Spanish lab, she thought about how supportive Gina had been for the past few weeks and knew her friend would be excited, too. From a distance, Hallie saw Gina talking with the other club members in the hall. She smiled and picked up her pace.

Gina was clearly focused on her conversation. One of the club members had mentioned how much attention the play's cast had been getting at school lately. A few other kids moaned in agreement, and that was enough to set Gina off. She launched into a tirade about Hallie and what a bore she'd become.

"All she ever talks about is that stupid play," Gina said. "Someone needs to tell her—and the rest of those drama geeks—that this is not Broadway. It's a stupid little play at a stupid little middle school. Nobody cares!"

Gina's comments got some giggles, and that made her feel good. She enjoyed venting about Hallie—not to mention making the other kids laugh—so she kept going.

Talk About It

- **Do you think Gina likes Hallie anymore? Why or why not?**

- **Have you ever been so frustrated with a good friend that you talked about her behind her back? Did it make you feel better or worse?**

Gina's back was to Hallie, so Hallie started sneaking up to surprise Gina. A couple of other kids' eyes widened when they saw Hallie. One gestured to Gina, trying to interrupt her. But it was too late. Hallie came up behind Gina just in time to see Gina twirling her hair and striking an overly dramatic pose. Gina said, "My name is Hallie, and I'm an *actor* in the school play! The whole cast is just *divine*, and I'm told my performance is simply *brilliant*. I've been offered my own television show, and—"

Gina stopped short when she noticed that nobody was laughing. Slowly, she turned around, pretty sure she knew who she'd see. Hallie was right there behind her. She'd heard every word of Gina's cruel impression.

"Hallie!" Gina exclaimed. "I didn't mean anything by it. You know that! We were just having some fun." But Gina was too late. The damage was done. Hallie turned and hurried away.

Talk About It

- Have you ever been caught trash talking about a friend? Were you sorry you'd done it or just sorry you were caught?

- Have you ever caught a friend talking trash about you? What did you do?

- Why did Hallie leave the scene so fast? How would you have handled the situation if you were in Hallie's shoes?

Gina watched her friend disappear down the hall. One of her Spanish Club friends whispered, "Awkward." Gina felt completely ashamed. Hallie hadn't done anything to deserve this. Not really. She'd just been excited. Gina knew Hallie would have cut back on the play talk if she'd asked her to.

Gina watched her friend disappear down the hall.

Gina wondered if Hallie would ever forgive her. She hoped so. Just the thought of not being friends with Hallie made her very, very sad. And she knew she only had herself to blame if Hallie never spoke to her again. How could she have been so careless?

Talk About It

- **Why didn't Gina tell Hallie about what had been bothering her?**
- **What advice would you give Gina about approaching Hallie after the incident?**
- **Would you forgive Gina if you were Hallie?**

Ask Dr. Robyn

Trash talking about a friend can seem like an innocent way to blow off steam. Well, as Gina's story illustrates, trash talking can end up hurting both the friend being ridiculed and the girl doing the talking. This is true even if the trash talker doesn't get caught in the act. Besides damaging the reputation of the person you're bashing, you also damage your own reputation. People see you as someone who says mean things at a friend's expense. Even if they laugh or join in, they may assume that if you'll do that to a friend, you'll do that to them when they're not around.

We all get upset with our friends. But taking out your frustrations on a friend by talking behind her back is unfair. Saying unkind things rarely makes you feel better for very long, and it never solves the real problem you're facing. If you ever find yourself in Gina's shoes, the most mature thing you can do is to talk things over with your friend. Be honest about what's bothering you, and give her a chance to work through the drama with you face-to-face.

Get Healthy

1. If you're frustrated with a friend, take a moment to reflect on your relationship. Remind yourself why you're close. Mentally list some of your friend's good qualities. Then decide how you can constructively address the problem by talking with your friend, not behind her back.

2. Whenever you're tempted to lash out at a friend, put yourself in her shoes. Does your friend even know what's bothering you? If not, calmly tell her about it.

3. Make an effort to be patient with friends who are pursuing activities you're not a part of. When a friend is excited and deeply involved with something, let her talk, even if she goes on a bit too long. She will appreciate your support and give it back to you when you need it.

The Last Word from Lisa

Communication between friends is a constant game of give-and-take. At various times in any friendship, one of you will inevitably give more than you take. The trick is learning to expect such periods of inequality and not let them ruin your friendship. Do your friendship a favor and treat your friend the way you expect her to treat you: No trash talking allowed!

3

Mixed Feelings

navigating the girl-boy friendship can be tough at any age, but it can be especially difficult when you're young and just starting to expand your circle of friends. The girl-boy friendship can be one of the most rewarding relationships you'll form. It offers both parties a fresh take on the world, exposing them to ideas and insights that enrich their current lives and come in handy well into the future.

Despite what some people may think, it's absolutely possible to be good friends with a boy without things turning romantic. True, sometimes feelings crop up between the two of you that might be confusing. These feelings can last for just a second, or they might plague you for longer than you'd care to admit. But as long as you recognize your confusion, you can work through it (either by yourself or by talking with your friend) and get back to your clearheaded coexistence as friends.

For example, perhaps your good friend Joe suddenly asks you out. You had no idea that he liked you as anything more than a friend. It's confusing because you haven't thought about dating him. You really don't know how you feel about it! You wonder how you can handle it without hurting his feelings, and how you can quickly figure out how you really feel. Of course, you might know exactly how you feel. Maybe you have no interest whatsoever in changing the terms of your friendship. Or maybe you are interested. Either way, you know that your response may cause conflict.

Despite what some people may think, it's absolutely possible to be good friends with a boy without things turning romantic.

Let's consider another possible scenario: you and Joe both want to be "just friends." But perhaps you each occasionally feel jealous of the other one's romantic interest in someone else. This situation can feel confusing, too, and may pose a threat to your friendship if you don't keep the lines of communication open. As long as you pay attention to your feelings and keep talking to your friend, you can learn how to handle confusing feelings, just like Lulu did.

Lulu's Story

Lulu and Sean were best friends. They made each other laugh and helped each other cope with the difficult things in their lives. They talked about everything from tough classes to annoying siblings to their favorite movies. Lulu loved their easy friendship. Around Sean, she never had to censor what she said. She could be herself, and that was good enough for Sean.

Talk About It

- Do you have friends who let you just be yourself? How does that feel?

- Are your friendships with boys different from your friendships with girls? If so, how?

Some of Lulu's other friends teased her that Sean was her secret boyfriend, or that Sean thought Lulu was his girlfriend. But those things weren't true. Sean was her friend, and that was it. That was how Lulu felt, anyway, until one confusing day when Sean asked her for advice.

"You've got to help me out, Lulu," Sean said. "Ever since Melanie became my science partner, I've really started to like her."

"Oh, Melanie's nice," Lulu said. "I like her a lot."

"That's good to know. But what I mean is, I *like her*," Sean said.

Lulu hadn't expected to hear that. She felt like she'd been pierced in the heart. And she suddenly felt flushed and too uncomfortable to look Sean in the eye.

Talk About It

- Why do you think Lulu felt so uncomfortable when Sean told her that he liked Melanie?

- Have you ever been uncomfortable while talking to a guy you know well? What was going on?

Sean went on, not noticing Lulu's changed demeanor. "She's so pretty, and she's smart, too. But all we ever talk about is science class. I can't tell if she likes me that way. Sometimes I think so, maybe. Then I think she probably just thinks I'm funny. I don't know what to do. What do you think?"

"Oh, I see," Lulu said. She wondered if Sean noticed her voice wavering. "You want me to help you with Melanie? Like, see if she's interested in you?"

"Yeah, kind of," Sean said, still oblivious to Lulu's discomfort. "I was hoping you could tell me what to say. Maybe you could talk to Melanie and see what she thinks of me. I trust you."

"I was hoping you could tell me what to say. Maybe you could talk to Melanie and see what she thinks of me. I trust you."

Lulu thought back to last year when she had helped Sean meet a different girl. Nothing really came of it for Sean. The girl was in the class above them.

She thought Sean was nice, but she didn't see him as boyfriend material, or really anything more than someone to say hi to in the hallway. Sean had bounced back just fine. Every once in a while, he and Lulu still laughed about his failed "love."

Talk About It

- Why do you think Sean didn't notice that Lulu was uncomfortable?

- Have you ever asked a friend (boy or girl) to talk to a crush on your behalf? What was your friend's reaction? Did it help or hurt the situation?

But this time, Lulu didn't feel like helping Sean. She didn't want Melanie to like him. And furthermore, she didn't want Sean to like Melanie. She wondered what was wrong with her. For a moment, Lulu wanted Sean to like *her*. And that felt really weird.

Things between Lulu and Sean turned awkward for a few days. Lulu could barely talk to Sean. She thought her feelings must be written all over her face. Sean didn't know what was going on. He couldn't figure out what had happened. All he knew was that Lulu was acting strangely and doing her best to avoid him. Things between them had definitely changed.

Lulu thought things through over the weekend. She realized that she didn't have a crush on Sean as she'd feared. She'd just been surprised that he had a new crush, and she felt a little jealous. Actually, she felt *a lot* jealous! She knew she had to break the ice. So she sent Sean a text. She apologized for being weird lately and asked if they could talk after school on Monday. To her relief, Sean texted right back with a simple, "Hey. Nice 2 finally hear from u. Movie tomorrow. 4pm."

Lulu looked at her cell and smiled. That felt right. She was sure now that things could get back to normal.

In fact, Lulu was pretty sure that she and Sean would have a good laugh about everything that happened—whenever she decided to come clean with him about her moment of jealousy!

Talk About It

- What should Lulu tell Sean about how she's been acting? Does he need to know that she was jealous of his crush on Melanie?

- Have you ever been jealous of a boy's crush on someone else? If so, why do you think that happened? How did you deal with it?

- What's the best way to handle confusing feelings in a girl-boy friendship?

Lulu was surprised by her intense feelings of jealousy. She was not romantically interested in Sean, so it was very confusing for her. It made her wonder if maybe she did like Sean in that way. She probably felt a little guilty about her feelings too, because they were keeping her from being a true friend to Sean.

When you suddenly don't know how you feel about a friend of the opposite sex, it's normal to react with embarrassment. A natural impulse is to avoid him so that you don't have to deal with it. But if you want to keep the friendship, you must deal with it. You owe it to yourself and to your friend to either work through your feelings on your own or to talk to him and let him in on the problem.

Talking to your friend can help clear the air. If you find yourself in a situation similar to Lulu's, it will take some courage to admit your mixed feelings. But doing so will ensure that you are both on the same page in the relationship. You can reaffirm that you are friends who trust each other enough to have the occasional uncomfortable conversation.

Get Healthy

1. When confusing feelings hit, don't feel guilty. You've done nothing wrong. Feelings

of friendship and romantic love can easily be mistaken for each other during stressful or unexpected situations. The key is to acknowledge your feelings as they happen and get to the bottom of them.

2. Telling a friend that you're jealous of his crush on another girl sounds mortifying. But it doesn't have to be. Approach your admission with good humor. With a laugh you could say something like, "I was kind of getting used to being the favorite girl in your life." If you don't make a big deal out of it, he won't either.

3. Talk about your jealousy with a trusted girl-friend. Let her help you sort out your feelings before you say or do anything you'll regret.

The Last Word from Lisa

At this age, the girl-boy friendship is almost bound to result in drama of some kind. When you experience mixed feelings, a good strategy is to identify exactly what caused them. If your reaction to those feelings causes conflict or tension between you and your friend, it's up to you to address the situation. You need to take ownership of any problem you've caused and provide an explanation for what happened. You can do it—and it will be okay!

4

Different Families

One constant in any friendship is the unique perspective each friend brings to the relationship. While many friendships form on the basis of shared interests or ideas, no two people have lived exactly the same life. In other words, you are the product of your own set of experiences, and so is any friend you know. Perhaps you come from a large family and your friend has a small one. Maybe she has moved around a lot but you've been in the same apartment all your life. You might have two parents in your life while she has one—or even several. Or maybe your two families are of different races or religions. You get the idea.

Without any differences, a friendship can quickly become boring. After all, it's no fun to hang out with an exact replica of yourself—not for long, anyway! But sometimes differences between friends can cause drama. Sticky situations can arise, for example, when two friends have been raised with different sets of rules and expectations. It might take awhile for these differences to become clear, but when they do, conflict can quickly follow. Chandra and her friend Kirsten were one such set of friends.

Chandra's Story

Whether she was at home with her family or out with her friends, 13-year-old Chandra knew the rules her parents expected her to follow. Conflicts came up now and then about extending curfew or how much time she spent online, but Chandra usually had little trouble following the rules.

Chandra's good friend Kirsten was another story. Kirsten made up her own rules. Her parents gave her the freedom to come and go as she pleased. She could hang out with kids her parents hadn't met. She could bring home low grades. From Chandra's perspective, Kirsten did whatever Kirsten felt like doing . . . whenever Kirsten felt like doing it.

Without any differences, a friendship can quickly become boring. After all, it's no fun to hang out with an exact replica of yourself—not for long, anyway!

Talk About It

- Would you describe your upbringing as closer to Chandra's or Kirsten's?

- How do you think Chandra feels about the rules in her own home? How do you think she feels about the rules in Kirsten's home?

As the girls got older, their different styles became more noticeable. After school, Chandra usually practiced her oboe and did her homework so she would have lots of free time after dinner. Kirsten would head straight to the mall after school, play video games until it was late, and then call or text Chandra in the middle of the night to see if she'd let her copy the next day's history homework.

More and more, Chandra felt conflicted about how to handle her friendship with Kirsten. She loved her friend. But she didn't always want to do everything Kirsten did. They had such different ideas about what was fun. Chandra felt increasingly uneasy with some of Kirsten's choices. They didn't always fit her own notion of what was right.

More and more, Chandra felt conflicted about how to handle her friendship with Kirsten.

Talk About It

- Why do you think Chandra doesn't want to do everything Kirsten does?

- What might Kirsten think about the way Chandra lives her life?

- Do you think girls with such different sets of rules can maintain a friendship? Why or why not?

One night, the pair went to a high school basketball game and cheered on the team. At halftime, Chandra saved their seats while Kirsten went to the concession stand for sodas. But instead of drinks,

Kirsten brought back two high school boys. Chandra was polite when Kirsten introduced them. But she spent the rest of the game talking to other friends while Kirsten flirted with the guys.

When the game ended, Kirsten told Chandra the guys had offered to drive them home. Chandra was surprised and a little nervous.

Chandra pulled Kirsten aside. "This is a bad idea," she said. "We don't even know them."

"Come *on*, Chandra," Kirsten begged. "Don't be like that. They seem perfectly nice to me! We need a ride, they have a car. What's the problem?"

Talk About It

- **Why do you think Chandra feels nervous?**

- **How would you handle this situation if you were Chandra?**

"I thought your mom was picking us up," Chandra said.

"She won't come unless I call," Kirsten said.

"Kirsten," Chandra said, "this isn't safe. Do these guys even live in this city? Do they know how much younger we are? I'm not riding home with them, and I won't let you either. The answer is no."

"You can't be serious," Kirsten said, rolling her eyes. "Grab your coat. They're waiting."

"I'm telling you," Chandra said. "My parents would kill me if I got in that car. You know I'm not going to freak out, but I'm not going with you either."

"But you *are* freaking out!" Kirsten exclaimed.

"Look," Chandra replied, "you can call your mom like we planned or you can leave me behind. If you leave, I'll call your mom myself . . . and then I'll call my parents. You know them. They'd get the police to come looking for you. And I might be happy if they did."

Kirsten looked back and forth between Chandra and the guys. The boys were getting impatient.

Chandra wasn't bluffing. With a sigh Kirsten turned to the boys and said, "Hey, it was nice to meet you, but my friend and I have other plans. See you around!"

Talk About It

- **What do you think about Kirsten's response to Chandra's ultimatum?**

- **Have you ever refused to do something a friend wanted because it was against your rules? What was the situation, and how did it turn out?**

Chandra was relieved that Kirsten had chosen to stay with her—but she was even more surprised at the decision. She raised her eyebrows at Kirsten, waiting to see what she would say.

Kirsten didn't say anything though. She just stood there with her arms crossed.

Chandra sighed and said, "I think we have some things to figure out. I mean, we're totally different. Do we really want to fight about this kind of stuff?"

"No," Kirsten said. "Let's talk about it later. I guess I'd better call my mom."

Talk About It

- Are you surprised that Kirsten backed down and chose to do what Chandra wanted?

- What did you like about the way Chandra handled the situation? Would you have done anything differently?

- Do you think Chandra and Kirsten will be able to stay friends despite their differences?

Chandra and Kirsten were raised with very different rules and expectations. Even so, they found enough common ground to become great friends. Their upbringings influenced their behaviors. For example, Chandra liked to play it safe while Kirsten was prone to taking risks.

If, like Chandra, you've experienced conflict with a friend related to your different upbringings, you can probably understand her frustration. She wanted to watch out for Kirsten, and she wished Kirsten would act more responsibly. Kirsten, on the other hand, didn't want to be held back. She wished Chandra would be more spontaneous and fun.

When two friends have been raised with different ideas about appropriate behavior, they are bound to clash sometimes. The hope is that in the heat of any drama they can listen to each other's perspectives and reach a compromise they can both live with. While it is okay to be free-spirited, if your friend is worried about you, there's a good reason to take a step back. Listen to your friend and think before you make a decision you might regret.

Get Healthy

1. If you think your friend is about to do something unsafe, trying to stop it is always the right thing to do.

2. Don't give in to peer pressure. You never have to take part in any activity that you think is wrong. Trust your instincts. If something makes you uncomfortable, there is usually a reason.

3. If your friend is trying to stop you from doing something she wouldn't do, honor your friendship by listening to what she has to say. You may discover that your friend has a good point.

4. Be respectful of a friend's different upbringing. "Different" does not necessarily mean "bad" or "wrong."

The Last Word from Lisa

As you get older, it's important for you to always think for yourself and do what is truly best for your well-being. If a friend has different ideas about fun or safe activities, it's up to you to voice your thoughts and use your best judgment. In the end, your friend may do the opposite of whatever you wish she'd do. But at least you'll know that you kept her best interests in mind, and that's an important trait in any friend.

5

Parent Issues

Parents are the glue that keeps families together. Most parents are very concerned about their children's well-being. But parents are human, too. Just like you, they make mistakes. And some of those mistakes might affect you in ways you don't want to deal with.

Sometimes, for example, your parents might unfairly assume that you've done something wrong before gathering all the facts. (Can you think of any instances where you've done the same thing?) Other times, they might be under huge amounts of adult-level stress and temporarily take out some of that on you. What if, for example, they want you to stop being friends with someone only because they dislike your friend's parents?

Maintaining a friendship when your parents disapprove can be tough. This type of situation puts you squarely in the middle. You feel like you must choose between your family and your friend. That can hurt when you want to choose both without losing either. Zoe's parents put her in the middle, and it was really starting to take its toll.

Zoe's Story

Zoe and Sarah were longtime friends. They'd grown from having playdates and sleepovers to being fixtures at each other's family events.

Around the time Zoe and Sarah started sixth grade, Zoe noticed her parents steering her away from Sarah. They didn't come right out and tell Zoe not to be friends with her. But they clearly had some kind of problem with Sarah's parents. And it was affecting how they viewed and treated Sarah.

Around the time Zoe and Sarah started sixth grade, Zoe noticed her parents steering her away from Sarah.

It didn't take long for Zoe to figure out what was going on. Her parents worked hard to provide for their family. But household finances had gotten tight that year after Zoe's mom was laid off from her job. Some months, the family struggled just to get by. Zoe had noticed that her parents were extremely sensitive about

their family's financial situation. They had to cancel their annual trip to the lake, and her parents didn't want anyone to know about it. Whenever Zoe brought up money, they got defensive and changed the subject. Compared to Zoe's parents, Sarah's were wealthy, and Zoe's parents seemed to resent them for it.

Talk About It

- Why are Zoe's parents trying to steer her away from Sarah? Will that benefit anyone?

- Have your parents ever disapproved of a friend's family? How did it affect your friendship?

Sarah still came over to Zoe's house. The girls would watch television or a DVD Sarah brought with her. Sometimes, Sarah would show up out of the blue to drop off an "extra" casserole or dessert from home. Once, she even brought Zoe a new outfit. She said it didn't fit her and she couldn't return it.

Zoe's parents seemed to appreciate those gestures the first few times. But then they asked Sarah to stop bringing things. Zoe and Sarah sensed Zoe's parents were embarrassed, as if it felt like charity to them.

Talk About It

- **Do you think Zoe and Sarah are aware of what is going on? Do you think they should talk about it?**

- **How do you think the awkwardness between the girls' parents might affect their friendship—now and in the future?**

The families' different lifestyles hadn't seemed to matter before. But after the layoff it seemed as if Zoe's parents hated Sarah's parents—and maybe even Sarah—for not being poor. They hinted that Zoe should see less of Sarah. And they started saying unkind things about Sarah's parents. They called them snobs, said they spoiled their children, and complained that Sarah's family thought they were "lower-class citizens."

Zoe didn't know how to handle this. She stuck up for Sarah whenever she could. Usually, her parents would have to agree when she'd point out how hard Sarah's family worked, how nice they'd always been, and that Sarah was a great friend who never acted selfish or spoiled.

Sarah worried about it, too. The tension surrounding her visits to Zoe's house was clear. Zoe was embarrassed by her parents' behavior. Sarah was embarrassed that she had "more" than Zoe. She felt hurt that Zoe's parents seemed to hold her responsible for it. Reluctantly, the girls started limiting their time together. They talked at school, but that was about it.

Talk About It

- How do you think Zoe feels about what her parents say about Sarah's family?

- Do you think Zoe's parents realize that they are causing problems between Zoe and Sarah? Why or why not?

- Are Zoe's parents being fair to Sarah and her family? Why or why not?

The situation went from bad to worse when Sarah's mom invited Zoe on their family vacation to the beach. Sarah's mom came to talk with Zoe's mom. The conversation went fine until Sarah's mom said that Zoe deserved a fun spring break after all she'd been through that year. That's when Zoe's mom hit the roof. She said "Absolutely not!" to the invitation and insisted that her kids were doing just fine without pity from rich snobs. She also said that Sarah wasn't welcome in their home anymore.

Zoe was mortified. She didn't want her friendship with Sarah to end over some stupid problem her parents had.

Zoe was mortified. She didn't want her friendship with Sarah to end over some stupid problem her parents had. She vowed to talk to Sarah at school the next day and come up with a plan.

Zoe knew that she needed to talk to her parents, and somehow she'd have to get her parents to apologize. But the first thing she wanted to do was make sure that Sarah was still speaking to her.

The next day at school, Zoe approached Sarah at her locker. Before Zoe could even say anything, Sarah smiled at her and gave her a big hug. "I know things are tough at home right now," Sarah said, "but I'm here for you, okay?"

Zoe was overwhelmed with emotion. She felt torn between her friend and her family, but Sarah's support made her feel like maybe things were going to turn out all right. Now she just had to talk to her parents.

Talk About It

- Would you blame your friend for something one of her parents did?

- What advice would you give Zoe about talking to her parents?

- How can Zoe and Sarah overcome this problem and stay friends?

Zoe was caught in a difficult tug-of-war between what her parents seemed to want and what she wanted. Zoe was torn because she understood why her parents were reacting this way toward Sarah's family. She saw that they were struggling, and it was pretty clear to her that those frustrations were clouding their judgment. Zoe had the right idea to try to talk with her parents about what was going on. She also needed to reach out to Sarah to let her know that they were still friends.

When parents make mistakes that affect your friendships, it's okay to tell them how you feel. If you're upset and you think they've been unfair, or they've done something to embarrass you, they need to know so you can address the issue together. They will have to decide what to do from there, whether they apologize for overreactions or ease up on their restrictions toward your friend. But as long as you keep the dialogue going with them—and your friend—you stand an excellent chance of being able to resolve the conflict.

Get Healthy

1. Don't shut out your parents when you find yourself at odds with them. Talk to them about what's bothering you.

2. Apologize to your friend about your parents' actions when you think they've done something wrong. Let her know that you want to resolve the problem and stay friends.

3. Give your parents a break if you know they're under stress. Assume that they will want to reexamine the situation once they've calmed down. Then give them a chance to take responsibility for any conflict they've caused.

4. Make sure your friends know how you feel about them. Any day's a good day to tell a friend why you like her.

The Last Word from Lisa

Let's face it: you probably won't be able to make it out of your teen years without your parents disapproving of at least one friend you bring home. Sometimes they'll have good reason to disapprove. But when they don't, tell your parents why you don't agree with them. If you think they've unfairly criticized a friend or a friend's family, your opinion matters. Really listen to what your parents have to say on the issue. That will make them want to listen to you, too. And, as always, keep talking to your friend. Two heads are better than one, and this is a perfect time for you to work together toward the goal of a lasting friendship.

6

Starting Rumors

Misunderstandings are a fact of life. Unfortunately, we all get caught up in them from time to time with family, teachers, strangers, and even our closest friends. Whenever communication occurs, the potential for misunderstanding exists. We each hear things in a unique way, and we interpret what we hear based on our own experiences and perspective. Communication breakdowns in the form of incorrect interpretations of another person's words or actions can happen between any two people. And these can lead to conflict, especially when we fail to view the situation from the other person's point of view.

When misunderstandings happen between you and a friend, one or both of you may feel hurt. In some cases the resulting conflict can turn serious. So serious, even, that one of you decides to end the friendship. The friend who's been left behind may decide to retaliate. Sometimes spreading rumors seems like one of the most effective ways to get back at someone who has upset you. But like Janie, you'll learn that just isn't the truth.

Janie's Story

Janie was shocked when Nell said their friendship was over. Sure, they'd had an argument—a silly one. Janie had been upset, thinking that Nell hadn't returned the art book she'd lent her. Nell told Janie she'd given it back two weeks ago. Janie said no way, she never got it. Nell, however, was able to prove that she'd left the book with Janie's mom when Janie wasn't home. It turned out that Janie's mom had put it on a shelf and had forgotten to mention it. It was all a big misunderstanding.

Janie apologized, but Nell refused to forgive her. Nell said she simply could not be friends with *anyone* who called her a liar.

Janie apologized, but Nell refused to forgive her. Nell said she simply could not be friends with *anyone* who called her a liar. Janie was hurt by Nell's decision. She was angry, too, especially because a few other girls supported Nell's position.

Talk About It

- Have you ever had a misunderstanding with a friend? How did the disagreement make you feel?

- Have you ever ended a friendship with someone? What made you end the friendship instead of trying to work it out?

- Is ending the friendship a reasonable thing for Nell to do?

Janie decided to teach her ex-friend a lesson. Lots of their friends had heard them fighting about the book, but few knew that they'd figured out what had happened. So Janie started a rumor that Nell had finally returned the book once she'd been caught trying to keep it for herself.

Janie told a guy in their class that Nell liked to steal things. She told their friend Anne that she never would have suspected Nell of taking the book if she didn't already know that Nell had a problem with stealing. Janie hinted that people should keep their valuables away from her. Janie said Nell had a problem and had started to shoplift at a discount store. She told a convincing story and included details about trying to help Nell. She also told her classmates how upset Nell's parents were about the situation. Even some of Nell's closest friends believed Janie's tale.

Talk About It

- Does Janie have a right to be angry with Nell for ending their friendship? Why or why not?

- What do you think about Janie's decision to start a rumor about Nell? Is there ever a good reason to start a rumor about someone?

The rumor spread all over school. When Nell heard about it during gym class, she marched straight over to Janie.

"Take it back," Nell demanded.

"Oh, hi, Nell," Janie said. "So you're talking to me again?"

"Just this one time—to tell you to *take it back*," Nell said. "Everyone is talking about me. I know you started it."

"I'd help you if I could," Janie said. "But I have no idea what you're talking about."

As Nell moved in closer, Janie took a step back. She had expected Nell to be angry, but not *this* angry.

Talk About It

- Why do you think Nell is so angry at Janie? Is she mad about the rumor itself, or is she upset about the fact that Janie started it?

- Has a former friend ever spread a rumor about you? How did you handle it?

"Take it easy, Nell," Janie said. "Nobody really believes you're a thief. We're all just kidding around. You know how these things go—everyone will be talking about something else tomorrow."

"Is that supposed to make me feel better?" Nell asked. "I'm the biggest joke in school right now!"

"You deserved it," Janie said. "You turned your back on me over one stupid little argument. I'm still really mad at you."

"How could you possibly be mad?" Nell questioned. "We were supposed to be friends. Yet you automatically accused me of stealing your book. You called me a liar. And you have the nerve to be mad at me? Unbelievable."

"You deserved it," Janie said. "You turned your back on me over one stupid little argument. I'm still really mad at you."

"But I apologized," Janie protested, "and you refused to accept it. A real friend would have said it was okay when the other one said she was sorry.

That really hurt. You made me feel like we'd never really been friends at all."

"That's how you made me feel," Nell said. "A real friend wouldn't start such a mean rumor. Yeah, you apologized, but *only* for being wrong about the book. You never once said you were sorry for thinking I was a liar."

Talk About It

- **What do you think about Nell's point that Janie never apologized for thinking she was a liar?**

- **Why do you think it took so long for Nell to tell Janie why she was really hurt?**

- **Do you think the two girls will be able to work out their argument?**

In that moment, Janie knew Nell was right. She hadn't put herself in Nell's shoes before. She'd been wrong to jump to conclusions about her friend's motives. And she finally understood why Nell felt so hurt.

Janie apologized again—for real this time— about the entire book fiasco and for starting such a mean rumor. She promised to tell everyone that she'd made it up. And from the look on Nell's face, Janie was pretty sure she'd gotten it right this time.

Talk About It

- Why is this apology different from Janie's first apology? What makes it more real?

- Should Nell forgive Janie? Why or why not?

- Do you think Janie really understands why Nell was so upset in the first place? If so, what made her "get it"?

Janie's first mistake was accusing Nell of lying about the book. Janie automatically assumed that Nell had stolen the book simply because she hadn't seen it. Who wouldn't be upset by that accusation from a friend? Nell was certainly upset, and her anger caused her to abruptly end the friendship. Janie felt hurt. She should have looked for a way to resolve the conflict. But instead she retaliated by spreading a damaging rumor about Nell. Janie ignored the possibility that she may have been wrong. And she consistently failed to look at the situation from Nell's perspective.

The desire to be "right" in any disagreement is strong. But nobody is right all the time. The primary goal should always be to respectfully reach a resolution. The next time you and a friend argue, make a point to step into your friend's shoes. You should seek to understand her perspective before you try to make her understand yours. Really listen to what she's telling you. This way, you can work out your differences with all points of view respectfully considered and all the facts on the table.

Get Healthy

1. Trust your friend to tell you the truth. If you both think two completely different things have happened, look for ways you might be

mistaken instead of rushing to assume your friend is wrong or lying.

2. Before accusing a friend of wrongdoing, empathize with her. Look at the situation from her point of view.

3. When a friend hurts you, resist the temptation to get even. Break the cycle of hurt feelings and nasty attacks. Do something positive instead—something that makes you feel good.

4. Keep in mind that a person who spreads malicious rumors is often distrusted by others. If you choose to do it, you may be the one who ends up being disliked.

The Last Word from Lisa

Retaliation can seem like your only option when you've been hurt by a friend. Keep in mind, though, that you always have the option to step back and evaluate the situation before taking drastic measures you might regret. Put your friendship first, even in these tough moments. You can do that by trying to understand your friend's point of view. Why did she hurt you in the first place? Has there been a misunderstanding? If so, can the two of you straighten it out? Giving a friend the benefit of the doubt is so much easier than continuing a needless fight from which your friendship may never recover.

7

The Boy Stealer

For most kids your age, the world of serious dating is still a frontier of the future. Certainly, there's no rush to pair off right now. But some girls you know have probably started dating. You might even be one of them. While having a boyfriend can be lots of fun, some girls find out that it creates friendship drama they never bargained for. An example is when one friend steals another's boyfriend.

Boyfriend stealing can happen fast and be a surprising turn of events for everyone involved. You may never be involved in this situation, but someone in your circle of friends surely will be. Having a friend betray you in this way is heartbreaking. Yet you can face the situation with your head held high. Breaking up with a boyfriend does not mean you are any less of a person, even if he left you to be with your best friend. It won't be easy, but once the drama dies down, you and your friend will need to figure out whether the friendship can survive. Amber and her friend Riley experienced this exact situation. Read on to see what happened.

Amber's Story

Amber was so excited to have her first boyfriend. She and Juan had been dating for about three weeks, and things were going really well. They were great friends, and she really enjoyed being around him.

Juan had been super understanding recently when Amber's good friend Riley tagged along on a Saturday date. The three of them talked and laughed over pizza. Amber was happy that Juan was so nice to her friend. She asked Juan to tell Riley about the time he'd seen Riley's favorite television star on a flight to Los Angeles. Riley was impressed and asked Juan for details. Amber just sat back and smiled. She was glad they all could have such a good time together.

Breaking up with a boyfriend does not mean you are any less of a person, even if he left you to be with your best friend.

Monday at school, Riley ate lunch with Amber and Juan. And for the next couple of days, Riley

regularly showed up at Amber's locker to chat between classes. This was unusual, but Amber didn't mind. She thought it was cute that Riley always asked if Juan would be stopping by. She even joked to her mom that she was starting to feel like the third wheel whenever Riley and Juan started talking.

On Friday, Amber canceled a date with Juan after learning she had to babysit her brother. She was disappointed. She'd barely seen Juan in the past few days. He said he'd been swamped with homework and some big student council project she'd never heard of. Amber hated calling to back out on their plans. But Juan quickly said, "Don't worry! It's been so crazy—I'd rather just crash at home tonight anyway."

"Call me tomorrow?" Amber said.

"Um, I don't know if I can," Juan said. Amber thought he sounded a little weird, but she figured he was probably just tired. "Let's just talk again at school on Monday, okay?"

Amber agreed. After all, they didn't need to be joined at the hip like some couples she knew. She told Juan to have a great weekend. Then she called Riley. If she didn't know better, she would have sworn that Riley sounded disappointed to hear her voice.

Talk About It

- Do you think Juan is hiding something from Amber? Why or why not?

- Why do you think Riley sounds disappointed to hear from Amber? Should Amber be concerned?

"Oh, uh, hi, Amber," Riley stumbled. "What's up? Have you talked to Juan today?"

"Yeah, we talked," Amber said. "I have to babysit tonight, and Juan is busy. Hey, what happened to you this week? At first I saw you five times a day and then, boom, you dropped off the face of the planet! Anyway, I'm calling to see if you want to do something tomorrow. Just us girls."

"That sounds great," Riley said. "I can't, though, because I'm—um—well—I'm—I'm grounded. I'm stuck at home. All weekend."

"Oh no, that's too bad," Amber said. "If I'm home tomorrow night, we could chat online if you want."

"Oh, uh, hi, Amber," Riley stumbled. "What's up? Have you talked to Juan today?"

"No!" Riley said. "I'm grounded from *everything*. In fact, I'd better get off the phone. Bye!"

Amber was surprised to get cut off. But she knew what it was like to be grounded. What she didn't know

was that both Juan and Riley had lied to her. They had started seeing each other during the past week. That was why they had both disappeared from Amber's sight. Juan was planning to break up with Amber on Monday, and then Riley was hoping to find a way to tell Amber that she was seeing Juan.

Talk About It

- **Is Amber too trusting of people? Do you think it is wrong that she trusts her best friend and boyfriend as much as she does?**

- **How does Riley feel about betraying her friend? How can you tell?**

The next day, Amber treated her brother to a matinee at the local movie theater. Even though she was sad that she couldn't hang out with Riley, she was glad to get out of the house and spend some time with her brother. But as they sat down in their seats, she saw something that made her look twice. She spied Riley and Juan ducking into the dark theater.

Amber was confused—until she saw her friend kissing her boyfriend. Then, she felt really angry. She stormed over. Right then, Amber almost didn't care about Juan. All she could think about was confronting Riley. When Juan saw Amber coming, he jumped up and ran out of the theater. Amber started crying as she yelled, "You lied to me and stole my boyfriend!" She turned away and ran up the aisle.

Riley called after Amber as she followed her out of the theater. "I never wanted to hurt you, I swear," Riley pleaded when she caught up with Amber in the lobby. "I didn't plan this. We were going to tell you on Monday."

Talk About It

- If your friend and your boyfriend started seeing each other behind your back, whose betrayal would hurt more? Why?

- Do you think it was right of Juan to run away? Whom should Amber be angrier with, Juan or Riley?

Still stunned, Amber said, "So that's why you suddenly started hanging around my locker, and then vanished just as quickly."

"It was wrong. I don't know what to say except I'm so sorry," Riley moaned.

"Really, Riley, I'd almost expect this from a guy, but you're my friend! Why couldn't you just wait until Juan broke up with me?" asked Amber.

"It's like I couldn't help it," Riley pleaded. "Amber, I really, really like him. I mean, I know it's bad. But you guys didn't go out for very long. I've been hoping it wouldn't matter to you too much. Do you hate me?"

Amber stood there staring at her friend. She felt absolutely humiliated. She was angry with Juan, but she was more hurt by Riley's betrayal. She looked Riley in the eye and said, "I just don't know, Riley. I need some time to think about this."

Talk About It

- Do you think Amber will be able to forgive Riley?

- What should Riley do to make it up to Amber? Can she make it up to her and save the friendship?

- How would you handle falling for your friend's boyfriend? Is it ever okay to act on such feelings? Is it okay that Riley did?

Amber had two tough decisions to make: whether she should forgive Riley and whether to continue their friendship. She felt confused because she and Riley had been close in the past.

Finding out that a friend has betrayed you is never easy. It's hard to make sense of it. How can one friend do something like that to another? You may not be able to salvage the relationship, but you have to decide whether it's worth a try. Is a boy more important than your friendship? Find out what led your friend to go behind your back this way. If you know her well, you can probably judge if she just got caught up in feelings she wasn't prepared to deal with or if she intentionally meant to hurt you. Attraction is a powerful force. It causes many rational people to behave in ways they normally wouldn't. That fact does not excuse deceitful behavior. However, keeping it in mind can help you look at the situation a little more objectively.

Get Healthy

1. If a friend betrays you, try not to blame yourself. Remember that your friend is responsible for what she did, not you.

2. If you find yourself attracted to a friend's boyfriend, stop and think about your friend. How would you feel if the tables were turned and she acted on her feelings? Is it worth it to risk your friendship over a guy?

3. Before betraying a friend (or anyone), think about what others will assume about your character. Will anyone trust you after this? What about the boy's character—will you trust him to stay loyal to you? What will you think about yourself if you act on this impulse? Let the answers to these questions guide your actions.

4. Talk to your parents about any overwhelming attraction you feel toward a boy. Sometimes just admitting that you don't know how to handle your feelings is enough for you to gain more control.

The Last Word from Lisa

Few girls set out to steal a friend's boyfriend. It's never okay to betray someone like that. Even though it can be hard to empathize with a friend who has done you harm, forgiving her is the only way the two of you can remain friends. Even if you go your separate ways, forgiveness is the best way for you to move on without feeling bitter and angry.

8

Abuse at Home

Nobody wants a friend to suffer for any reason. You probably cringe when you hear that a friend of yours has done poorly on a test, wrecked her brand-new snowboard, or gotten in a big fight with her parents. Most of the time, you can support a friend by doing simple things. You can cheer her up with a funny e-mail, bake her a special treat, or just lend an ear while she talks about whatever is bothering her.

There are times, though, when a friend's problem can be so serious that the support she needs may be something she doesn't want at the time. This can sometimes happen if you suspect a friend is being abused. Evidence might tell you that your friend is in trouble. You're not quite sure what to do, but you know you need to do something. It's going to be difficult, especially if your friend doesn't want to admit anything's wrong or have you get involved. There will definitely be drama, and you will have to make some hard decisions that might drive your friend away. But as Christina discovered, the hard decisions are well worth making.

Christina's Story

Christina's new friend Deanna was fun to have around. She was awfully accident-prone, though. She showed up at school with a new bump or bruise every week. Deanna always explained what had happened with tales of her own clumsiness. She'd reenact the scene, and pretty soon both girls would be in hysterics.

At first Christina thought Deanna's stories were funny. But after a while, Christina had trouble believing some of them. For example, Deanna said the bruises around her wrist were from catching her arm in the headboard while she slept. And her sprained ankle was from missing the last two basement stairs at home.

At first Christina thought Deanna's stories were funny. But after a while, Christina had trouble believing some of them.

Christina's mom had always told her to listen to her gut feelings about this kind of stuff—and her gut told her that something just wasn't adding up.

Talk About It

- Why does Christina think Deanna's stories don't add up?

- Have you ever thought a friend's explanations about something didn't ring true? What made you think so? Did you confront her about it?

Christina noticed other things, too. For instance, Deanna always wore long sleeves and high collars—even on warm days. She went out of her way to avoid going home. And she always had an excuse for why Christina couldn't visit her house.

From what she'd learned in health class, Christina suspected abuse. But what if she was wrong? Deanna always acted so cheerfully. Surely she'd ask for help if something like abuse were happening at home. Christina was afraid of embarrassing Deanna. So she decided to do nothing until she had more information. She could ask more questions the next time Deanna had an accident. Maybe she could even drop by Deanna's house unexpectedly to check things out.

Talk About It

- **Why does Christina think she will embarrass Deanna if she asks about her bruises? Why else might Christina be afraid to say anything?**

- **Do you think Christina has a responsibility to find out what's going on with Deanna? Why or why not?**

- **If Deanna is being abused at home, why isn't she confiding in her friend?**

Early one Saturday, Christina's cell phone rang. It was Deanna, and she asked if she could come over.

She apologized for calling so early but said her dad was already getting on her nerves.

"Sure, come on over," Christina said. "You'll have to watch me do laundry first, but after that we can hang out."

"Great," Deanna said. "I'll see you soon."

A couple of minutes later, the doorbell rang. Christina was still getting dressed, so she peeked out her bedroom window. Deanna was standing on the doorstep.

Christina opened the door and said, "That was fast! You must have called from right around the corner."

"I did," Deanna said. "Thanks for letting me come bug you today."

"It'll be great," Christina said. "Have you had breakfast? Why don't you take off your sunglasses and we can find something to eat."

Christina gasped as Deanna removed her sunglasses. Underneath was a horrible-looking black eye. "Deanna! Oh my gosh, what happened?" she asked.

Talk About It

- **What do you think happened to Deanna? Do you think she will tell the truth?**

- **Have you had a friend who always wanted to hang out at your house, and never at hers? Do you think she was avoiding something at home?**

"Oh, it's nothing," Deanna said with a nervous laugh. "You know me. Always walking into things. This time it was the screen door. No big deal."

Christina had a bad feeling that she couldn't ignore. Deanna's eye was in bad shape. It was the worst injury she'd seen on her yet. She remembered her teacher saying that sometimes signs of abuse get worse over time. She shook herself out of her thoughts and asked the question she'd been dreading.

"Deanna, you look like you've been punched in the face. Did someone hit you? Was it your dad? You can tell me anythi—"

"Are you crazy?" Deanna interrupted, clearly shaken. "Nobody hit me, you got that? I told you, it was just a silly accident."

"How exactly could the screen door cause that?" Christina pressed. "What were you doing?"

"You don't believe me?" Deanna said. "That's just great. I think I need to get out of here."

"No, don't go!" Christina said. "I believe you. But that eye looks just awful. Let me get my mom, and we can take you to see the doctor."

Christina paused for a moment. But she knew she had to try to help her friend, even if Deanna ended up hating her.

Deanna looked angry. "If you bring your mom into this, I swear I'll leave and you'll never see me again."

Christina paused for a moment. But she knew she had to try to help her friend, even if Deanna ended up hating her. She said, "I'm sorry, Deanna, I really am." Then she turned and yelled for her mom at the top of her lungs.

Talk About It

- Why does Deanna want to leave Christina's house?

- Do you think Christina and Deanna will stay friends after this?

- What should Christina tell her mom? How might Deanna handle the situation?

When Christina first suspected that her friend was in serious trouble, she did what many people would do in the same situation—she waited to see if her suspicions made sense. The possibility that a friend was experiencing abuse at home, whether it was physical, emotional, or verbal, was a scary prospect. It was only natural that Christina wanted to feel more certain of the situation before acting. But once she felt confident that something was wrong, she made the right move by going against her friend's wishes and summoning an adult. The problem was too big for Christina—or even Christina and Deanna—to handle alone.

Telling an adult about suspected abuse is daunting. When the suspected victim is your friend, you might feel especially helpless. You can't bear the thought of your friend being hurt, but you also worry about her reaction. She may be angry with you, and you might even lose the friendship, but her safety has to be your first priority.

Get Healthy

1. Educate yourself about the signs of abuse and where to get help. That way, you'll know what to do if a friend is in trouble.

2. Never be afraid to tell your parents or other trusted adult when you suspect a friend is being abused. They are in the best position to help.

3. Tell an adult about your suspicions even if your friend begs you not to. Her safety is the most important thing, even if she gets mad at you.

4. Be there for your friend if she needs to talk about her problems.

The Last Word from Lisa

We all need a friend's help from time to time. Some of those times are much more serious than others. They can be so serious that a friend in dire need may tell you to mind your own business and leave her alone. She may threaten to cut her ties with you entirely. It's important for you to understand that a friend who is being abused may not want you to know about it. She may feel embarrassed or ashamed, and she may fear that any questions will result in harm to her or others at home.

If a friend of yours is in trouble, you can bet that she needs your help, even if she won't admit it. The best thing you can do for her is to find a trusted adult to step in and assess the situation. He or she can take responsibility for finding your friend the most effective help.

9

Moving On

Kids probably move in and out of your neighborhood and school all the time. The moves can affect you in different ways. In some cases, in just a day or two it's almost like that person was never there. In others, you miss the person for a little while but don't exactly suffer. Life goes on.

Of course, the scenario that many kids dread is when a best friend moves away. Sometimes the friend who doesn't move ends up feeling lonely and lost. The sense of being left behind can grow when the friend who moved makes new friends. These obstacles can make it difficult for former best friends to stay connected. The distance alone makes it hard for old friends to maintain their close relationship. And having completely different experiences after the separation can make the distance seem greater. Muriel felt left behind when her friend Abby moved away. But she found that with a little work, long-distance friendships can turn out just fine.

Muriel's Story

Abby's mom had landed a great new job in a big city and had to relocate, so the entire family went along. Although Abby's best friend, Muriel, would still be in their small hometown, the girls vowed to stay best friends forever.

For a time the girls kept in touch every single day, just like always. They texted, e-mailed, called, and chatted online. Abby wanted to know all about what was going on at her old school. But things started to change as Abby settled into her new life. She met new people and started having all kinds of cool city experiences that Muriel couldn't relate to.

Meanwhile, Muriel was stuck back in her familiar town. Even though she had plenty of friends, she started to feel sorry for herself. It seemed to her that she had nothing new to do and nobody interesting to talk to. She felt lost and lonely without Abby. Muriel surprised herself one day when she realized she almost hated her friend for leaving her behind.

The distance alone makes it hard for old friends to maintain their close relationship.

Talk About It

- Has a best friend of yours ever moved away? How did that feel?

- In what ways might your daily life change if your best friend moved away?

- Have you ever blamed a friend for something that was out of her control, such as her family moving away?

One snowy Sunday, Muriel sat at home, gazing out the window and feeling sorry for herself. A group of friends had asked her to go to the mall with them, but she had turned them down. On days like this, she and Abby used to go sledding. Most of their other friends thought sledding was for little kids, but Muriel and Abby knew it was still awesome to speed down the hillside. They didn't care what others thought—they could make their own fun.

Muriel was sad because she and Abby hadn't communicated at all in the past week. That was a new record. Muriel knew Abby was really busy practicing for an ice-skating recital. So she just decided not to bother her.

Abby missed Muriel and wondered why she'd been silent all week. In truth, she *was* really busy and hadn't had a free moment to get in touch with Muriel. But because she was busy, she didn't spend as much

time thinking about how much she missed her friend. Muriel had been turning down invitations to hang out with friends because she felt sad. But all that extra time alone just made her think about how much she missed Abby.

Talk About It

- Why do you think Abby seems to be handling the separation better than Muriel?

- Have you ever been too busy to communicate with your best friends?

- Why do you think Muriel turned down her friends' invitations to hang out?

As Muriel pouted on the couch, her cell phone rang. It was Abby. Muriel felt happy for a second, but then she went back to feeling down. She answered using her most pathetic-sounding voice.

"Hey, Abby," Muriel said softly, almost like she was ill.

"Hi, Muriel," Abby said. "How've you been this week? I've missed you!"

"Sure you have," Muriel said.

"What?" Abby said. "Is something wrong?"

"Oh, it's nothing," Muriel said.

"Come on, Muriel," Abby said. "What's wrong? You sound like you don't even want to talk to me. What's going on?"

Muriel wondered what to say. It wasn't like Abby could fix the problem. She wouldn't move back to town, and Muriel wouldn't move to the city. How could the two of them keep up with the friendship from such a distance?

"I'm waiting," Abby teased. "You know you can talk to me about anything."

Talk About It

- Why is Muriel trying to sound pathetic on purpose?
- What does Abby do to let Muriel know she still cares? What else could she do?

Of course Muriel knew that she could talk to Abby about anything. It took a little courage, but finally she said, "I've been feeling really lonely lately, Abby. I want to be happy for you, but I'm a little jealous that you're having so much fun in your new city while I'm here without you. I really miss you."

"And I miss you too, Muriel!" Abby replied. "I mean, my friends here are really great, and I'm trying to like our new neighborhood, but it's just not the same. I'm actually jealous that you get to stay back with all our friends and do the same old stuff! I know we both feel lonely, but we're gonna get through this."

Muriel was so relieved that Abby understood. Muriel knew that she should hang out with their old friends more—the ones who hadn't moved away.

By spending so much time alone and feeling sorry for herself, Muriel realized that she had been dwelling on the past instead of creating new memories. Muriel was glad that she had been honest with Abby. It felt good to know that even though they didn't live near each other, they could still be close friends.

Talk About It

- **Are you surprised that Abby sometimes feels jealous of Muriel? Why or why not?**

- **Have you ever been hesitant to tell a friend about something that was bothering you? Did you ever open up? If so, what happened?**

"Have you been sledding yet?" Abby said. "I can't do that in the city."

"Who would go with me?" Muriel said. "Sledding is too uncool for our other friends—that's why I need my dorkiest friend back!"

Abby laughed and said, "Muriel, just call someone. Beth will go if you ask. And if she won't sled, do something else. I'll go sledding with you when we visit my grandparents next month."

"You never told me you were coming home! That's only a month away!" Muriel exclaimed. She couldn't believe that she would be able to see Abby again so soon.

"Yup. I was going to surprise you, but I couldn't wait to tell you. I've even got a countdown going on my cell phone. And when I get back, you'll be the first person I call."

Muriel hung up from the call feeling better. Abby would always be her friend, but she had to get used to the fact that Abby wasn't coming back. Muriel did have other friends, and it was time for her to act like it. Muriel took a deep breath and dialed Beth's number. Beth was shocked to hear from her—it had been awhile—but she was glad Muriel had called. And Muriel was, too.

> **Muriel did have other friends, and it was time for her to act like it.**

Talk About It

- **What part of Abby's advice do you think was most helpful to Muriel?**

- **Why do you think it took Muriel so long to reach out to another friend?**

- **Have you ever had to move on from seeing a best friend every day? What was that like? Were you able to stay friends in the long run?**

Ask Dr. Robyn

Losing a friend to a move can feel a lot like losing a friend for good. Even if you stay in touch, you know that things will never be the same. And that kind of loss can be difficult to take. Muriel, for example, felt that she had lost her other half. She wasn't sure what to do next and not sure she really wanted to do anything but sit at home and feel sorry for herself. But that made things even worse, because it caused her to dwell on her negative feelings instead of looking to the future. Once she shared her feelings with Abby, though, things started to look up. She saw that it was up to her to create her new reality.

When a friend moves away, you can form a new reality, and it can be a good one. But you will need to make the effort. All it takes is a willingness to open yourself up to other friendships and experiences. It is time to hang out with old friends and make new ones. Call upon your inner confidence to carry you through any uncertainty as you find your new routine. Redefine your friendship with the person who moved away. It can be fun to have the perspective of someone who isn't there every day—they can help solve problems and give advice without being in the thick of it.

Get Healthy

1. Talk to your friends about issues as they come up. Don't wait until you're feeling miserable and hopeless.

2. If you feel left behind after a friend moves away, don't isolate yourself. Reconnect with other friends and do anything else that gets you out of the house. Staying busy will help you to start making new memories.

3. If your friend is having a more difficult time with the separation than you are, help ease her transition. Discuss ways she can meet new friends.

4. Keep in touch with a friend who has moved away, but know that your friendship has to change. She can't stay involved in every aspect of your daily life. She can always be a good friend, though.

The Last Word from Lisa

If you and a best friend need to separate due to a move, see what you can do to minimize feelings of loneliness and loss. Instead of looking back, look forward to what you can gain. Plan when the two of you can talk or visit each other in person. Keeping your time together positive will help both of you adjust to the change.

A Second Look

Try as you might, you will never handle every instance of friend drama with perfect skill. Sometimes you will talk out of turn and say the right things at the wrong times. Maybe you'll even say the totally wrong things at the absolute worst times. Sometimes you will make faulty assumptions and bad decisions.

In short, you will occasionally fall down on the job as someone's friend. The good news is that you can always pick yourself back up. Where friendship exists, so does the potential for growth, understanding, and forgiveness. Friends are amazing—can you imagine life without them? Friendships are important as you are growing up and will be important throughout your life, so they are worth working on.

When you and a friend argue, you can work on resolving your issues using some of the simple strategies in this book. You can think twice before saying or doing something you'll regret. You can take a moment to really listen to your friend's concerns. You can empathize with each other. You can honor your friend's perspective by taking the time to understand it. And, when necessary, you can step in to help a friend when she needs help the most.

Now, go find a friend and thank her for being so special to you. It's always the right time to tell a friend how important she is in your life. Adopt the motto: More fun, less drama!

Lisa

Pay It Forward

Remember, a healthful life is about balance. Now that you know how to walk that path, pay it forward to a friend or even to yourself! Remember the Get Healthy tips throughout this book, and then take these steps to get healthy and get going.

• Making drastic changes may help you make a new friend, but if those changes are forced, you probably won't be able to sustain the friendship. Change can be positive, but change that leaves you wondering if you can ever be yourself again probably isn't worth it.

• The next time you hear someone talking trash, stand up for the person being insulted. Remind the speaker that her target isn't there to defend herself.

• When you feel yourself getting frustrated with a friend who only wants to talk about herself, speak up early, before you reach the boiling point. She may not realize what she's doing. Tell her with a chuckle that it's her turn to listen to you. She'll catch the hint, and you can avoid getting angry and starting an argument later.

• Make an effort to hang out in boy-girl groups so you can get better at interacting with boys and improving your communication skills.

- If you develop confusing feelings for a guy friend, write them out in the form of a letter or a journal entry. Writing things down can help you put your feelings in perspective. Put the writing away overnight and then revisit it the next day to see if you still have the same feelings.

- Remember that nobody, not even a good friend, can make you do something that makes you feel uncomfortable. Stand your ground when you need to. Respect yourself enough to do what you think is right.

- Make a weekly date to chat with your parents about your friends. Fill them in on what's happening at school and the kinds of things you and your friends talk about. Just keep it informal, and see where the conversations take you.

- Before taking an extreme measure such as ending a friendship, ask yourself what might be going on with the friend who has hurt you. Explore the possibility of working things out. If the friendship was worth having in the first place, isn't it worth saving?

- Make a pact with your best friend to always be honest with each other. That goes double for when you're experiencing conflict.

Additional Resources

Select Bibliography

Dellasega, Cheryl. *Surviving Ophelia: Mothers Share Their Wisdom in Navigating the Tumultuous Teenage Years.* New York: Ballantine, 2002.

Dellasega, Cheryl, and Charisse Nixon. *Girl Wars: 12 Strategies That Will End Female Bullying.* New York: Fireside, 2003.

Elman, Natalie Madorsky, and Eileen Kennedy-Moore. *The Unwritten Rules of Friendship: Simple Strategies to Help Your Child Make Friends.* Boston, MA: Little, Brown and Company, 2003.

Pipher, Mary. *Reviving Ophelia: Saving the Selves of Adolescent Girls.* New York: Ballantine, 1994.

Simmons, Rachel. *Odd Girl Out: The Hidden Culture of Aggression in Girls.* New York: Harcourt, 2002.

Further Reading

Desetta, Al, ed. *The Courage to Be Yourself: True Stories By Teens About Cliques, Conflicts, and Overcoming Peer Pressure.* Minneapolis, MN: Free Spirit Publishing, 2005.

DeVillers, Julia. *GirlWise: How to Be Confident, Capable, Cool, and in Control.* New York: Three Rivers Press, 2002.

Karres, Erika V. Shearin. *Mean Chicks, Cliques, and Dirty Tricks.* Avon, MA: Adams Media, 2004.

Simmons, Rachel. *Odd Girl Speaks Out: Girls Write About Bullies, Cliques, Popularity, and Jealousy.* New York: Harcourt, 2004.

Web Sites

To learn more about maintaining healthy friendships, visit ABDO Publishing Company online at **www.abdopublishing.com**. Web sites about maintaining healthy friendships are featured on our Book Links page. These links are routinely monitored and updated to provide the most current information available.

For More Information

For more information on this subject, contact or visit the following organizations.

Girl Scouts of the USA

420 Fifth Avenue, New York, NY 10018
800-478-7248
www.girlscouts.org
The Girl Scouts organization is dedicated to providing an environment of friendship and teamwork that helps girls build character and skills for success in the real world.

Prevent Child Abuse America

500 North Michigan Avenue, Suite 200
Chicago, IL 60611
312-663-3520
www.preventchildabuse.org
This organization builds awareness and provides leadership in the fight against abuse and neglect of America's children.

Glossary

abuse
Physical or psychological mistreatment.

betrayal
Disloyalty.

conflict
A disagreement or clash.

demeanor
A person's behavior, manner, or appearance, especially as it reflects his or her character.

drama
A situation that is particularly tense or emotionally involving.

empathize
To identify with and understand another person's feelings or difficulties.

expectation
A standard of conduct or performance required by or of somebody.

gossip
Often malicious conversation about personal rumors or facts.

misunderstanding

A failure to correctly interpret something.

perspective

The evaluation of a situation, facts, or attitudes according to one person's point of view.

retaliate

To deliberately harm another in response or revenge for a harm he or she has caused.

rumor

A generally circulated story or statement without facts that confirm its truth.

trash talking

To speak insultingly about a person or group.

ultimatum

A demand accompanied by a threat to inflict a penalty or punishment if the demand is not met.

upbringing

The way somebody has been raised or educated early in life.

Index

About the Author

Lisa L. Owens works as a writer and an editor from her home office near Seattle, Washington. After majoring in English and journalism at the University of Iowa, she worked briefly as a reporter before pursuing a career in children's publishing. Since the early 1990s, Lisa has worked on everything from award-winning social-emotional curricula to children's book reviews to graphic novels. As an author, she has published more than 60 works for children and young adults. She never tires of looking for new story angles and interesting information to share with her readers.

Photo Credits

Michael Chamberlin/Fotolia, 12; Galina Barskaya/Fotolia, 15; Tracy Whiteside/Shutterstock Images, 17; Monkey Business Images/Shutterstock Images, 23; D. Ducouret/Fotolia, 24; Michael Jordan/Fotolia, 27; Kristian Sekulic/Shutterstock Images, 33; Fotolia, 37, 75, 86; Konstantin Tavrov/Shutterstock Images, 43; Yuri Arcurs/Fotolia, 44; Jason Stitt/Shutterstock Images, 47; Shutterstock Images, 52; iStockphoto, 54, 66, 72, 89; Lorraine Swanson/Shutterstock Images, 57; Kevin Carden/Shutterstock Images, 63; Alexander Todorenko/Fotolia, 64; Rich Legg/iStockphoto, 77; Arsion Kireyau/Shutterstock Images, 80; Monika Wisniewska/Shutterstock Images, 84; Abby Wilcox/iStockphoto, 95; Donald R. Swartz/Shutterstock Images, 97